At Issue

Cell Phones and Driving

Other Books in the At Issue Series:

At Issue

| Cell Phones and Driving

Stefan Kiesbye, Book Editor

GREENHAVEN PRESS

A part of Gale, Cengage Learning

GALE
CENGAGE Learning™

Detroit • New York • San Francisco • New Haven, Conn • Waterville, Maine • London

Christine Nasso, *Publisher*
Elizabeth Des Chenes, *Managing Editor*

© 2011 Greenhaven Press, a part of Gale, Cengage Learning.

Articles in Greenhaven Press anthologies are often edited for length to meet page requirements. In addition, original titles of these works are changed to clearly present the main thesis and to explicitly indicate the author's opinion. Every effort is made to ensure that Greenhaven Press accurately reflects the original intent of the authors. Every effort has been made to trace the owners of copyrighted material.

Cover image © Images.com/Corbis.

LIBRARY OF CONGRESS CATALOGING-IN-PUBLICATION DATA

Cell phones and driving / Stefan Kiesbye, book editor.
      p. cm. -- (At issue)
   Includes bibliographical references and index.
   ISBN 978-0-7377-5145-1 (hardcover) -- ISBN 978-0-7377-5146-8 (pbk.)
   1. Cell phones and traffic accidents. 2. Distracted driving. 3. Traffic safety--United States. I. Kiesbye, Stefan.
   HE5620.D59C45 2011
   363.12'51--dc22

642001576   2010024370

Printed in the United States of America
1 2 3 4 5 6 7 14 13 12 11 10

Contents

Introduction

According to a recent study by the National Highway Traffic Safety Administration (NHTSA), 80 percent of all car accidents and 65 percent of near misses are caused by eating while driving. But while it has long been known that eating while driving distracts drivers, federal and state legislators have never banned the behavior. Indeed, drive-through eating is so ingrained in American culture that at this point it would be difficult, if not impossible, to do so. Some fear that if action is not taken quickly to ban cell phone use while driving, the outcome could be the same: people will become so used to driving while talking that banning the practice will be increasingly difficult.

The evidence against cell phone use in cars seems compelling. According to a 2008 NHTSA study, more than 800,000 drivers are using handheld devices at any one moment throughout the day. The NHTSA also notes that nearly 6,000 people a year are killed in accidents related to cell phone use while driving. The risks of driving while texting or talking on a phone has been demonstrated in numerous studies, and yet most people are unwilling to voluntarily give up talking while driving. Among other reasons, millions of people no longer have a landline and exclusively use a cell phone, and many people feel compelled to answer phone calls wherever they are, including in their moving vehicles.

If lawmakers want to curb cell phone use in cars, this might be an opportune moment. Many argue that the lesson of eating-while-driving is not that somehow people will find a way to safely multitask, or that lawmakers pick and choose their battles; rather, it is that once bad habits have a chance to develop and are seen as rights, it is almost impossible to outlaw them. Legislators today would most likely risk public outrage and their jobs should they attempt to wrest tacos and burgers from the hands of hungry drivers. But cell phone use, and especially texting-while-driving, is still—despite its wide use—in its infancy, and critics maintain that the present climate gives lawmakers the best chance to successfully ban these practices.

As technologies evolve and develop, allowing users ever-increasing access to electronic material on the go, the possibility of distractions will only increase. The following viewpoints present differing viewpoints on how the issue of cell phones and driving has been handled by lawmakers and others and on how it should be dealt with in the future.

1

Cell Phone Use Distracts Drivers

Edmunds.com

Edmunds.com publishes articles that engage and educate automotive consumers and enthusiasts and provides automotive industry commentary and analysis.

DWY—"driving while yakking"—has become the main distraction of drivers, thanks to cell phones that allow not only talking but also texting and the use of social-networking sites and e-mail. Studies have found that whether or not drivers use hands-free devices, they are severely distracted by ongoing conversations and are prone to ignore signs and signals and other traffic. While responsible cell phone use might cut back on the most fatal mistakes behind the wheel, the best choice is to shut off the phone and concentrate fully on the road.

At any given moment, more than 1 million U.S. drivers are talking on handheld cell phones, according to the National Highway Traffic Safety Administration (NHTSA). Why is this a problem? Cell phones (also called wireless phones) are a known distraction. In a 2008 survey by Nationwide Insurance, 67 percent of people admitted to using a cell phone while driving.

This has created an obvious concern about cell phone safety. Dozens of countries have banned the use of handheld phones while driving. In the U.S., California, Connecticut,

New Jersey, New York, Utah, Washington, D.C. and many municipalities have fully outlawed in-vehicle handheld phone use. Dozens of states have banned cell phone use by minors and bus drivers. Many other attempts at strong state legislation have failed or been tabled.

The Debate About Safety

At the core of this flurry of legislative attempts is the debate over whether DWY—or "driving while yakking"—is truly dangerous. Wireless-phone proponents say that talking on a cell phone is the same as or less of a distraction than changing your radio station, trying to control your kids or eating— none of which is regulated of course. Since many states already have laws that ban distracted driving, they contend that outlawing handheld cell phones is penalizing the technology instead of the behavior.

Driving while yakking is a distraction that may decrease our ability to operate the vehicle effectively.

A 2005 controlled study of Australian drivers found that cell phone users were four times as likely to get into an accident serious enough to injure them. These findings echoed the results of a 1997 study of Canadian drivers, who linked cell phone usage with increased property damage.

Whether we choose to admit it or not, driving while yakking is a distraction that may decrease our ability to operate the vehicle effectively. The Insurance Institute for Highway Safety (IIHS) analyzed the results of over 120 cell phone studies. They found that nearly all of the studies reported that some aspects of driver performance were affected by the mental distraction associated with cell phone use. The IIHS reported that phone conversation tasks typically decreased reaction times, travel speeds, and increased lane deviations and steering wheel movements.

Clearly, now that we have learned the benefits of cell phones, there's no going back. Instead of stewing in traffic, we can conduct business and stay in touch with family and friends. We can let people know when we're running late. If there's a problem on the road, cell phones allow us to call for roadside assistance or medical help. We can report problems: a drunk driver, a stranded motorist, an obstacle in the road. Drivers even call in traffic reports to radio stations, allowing the rest of the community to benefit from their knowledge.

Phones Pose a Great Risk

But let's face it. In spite of these benefits, cell phones do pose a serious risk because they distract from driving. With that in mind, here are our suggestions for using a cell phone safely in your car.

• Get to know your phone and its features—if you can dial a number with one key instead of seven or 10, you're better off.

• Position your phone within easy reach—bending over to reach for it takes your eyes of the road and can cause you to swerve.

• Suspend calls in heavy traffic or in bad weather—you need to focus even more under hazardous conditions.

• Do not take notes or look up phone numbers while driving—enough said.

• Keep conversations short. Inform the person you're calling that you are in a car, and hang up as soon as possible.

• If possible, place calls when you are not moving. Pull over where possible.

• Ask a passenger to help. Have someone else make or take the call.

• Do not engage in stressful or emotional conversations—leave the child support conversations for the home phone.

Hands-Free Phones?

One would think that using a hands-free phone would solve the problem. It leaves you with two hands on the wheel, right? Not necessarily. Most hands-free users are using some form of headphone or earphone. These often ill-fitting devices have frequent volume problems and can themselves be a source of distraction. The IIHS reported that a driver's likelihood of getting in an accident increases fourfold when talking on a wireless phone, whether handheld or hands-free. The NHTSA researched whether using phones hands-free makes a difference; it actually had to change its "test headphone" from an earclip design to a headband-style design (which runs over the crown of the head) to assure that test-drivers wouldn't have to use their hands to repeatedly adjust the earclips. The study found that drivers typically favored hands-free and voice-dialing options over holding the phone, and typically found these setups easier to use.

Most hands-free users are using some form of headphone or earphone. These often ill-fitting devices have frequent volume problems and can themselves be a source of distraction.

There are several hands-free options that make more sense, eliminating the need for a headphone by running voice calls through your car's speakers.

Additionally, an increasing number of cell phones and vehicles are equipped with Bluetooth technology. This allows you to have your phone anywhere in your car (even the trunk!) and still make and receive calls. You'll hear the calls through the speakers, and your voice will be transmitted through the car's built-in microphone. Bluetooth-enabled cars are equipped with voice recognition technology, such that you can make and receive phone calls without having to touch any buttons on the phone. . . .

What may come as an interesting surprise is that, even if a cell phone is being used completely hands-free, the risk of having an accident doesn't seem to be reduced. Apparently, the act of conversing on the phone—not holding the phone to your ear—is the more dangerous distraction. Emotional conversations in particular seem to elevate risk. So hands-free or not, there's an increased risk to DWY.

Even in states or localities where cell phones are banned, there is a serious problem with compliance.

Not Calling Might Be the Only Option

It is difficult to pinpoint exactly how many people are using hands-free devices. Most of the research has been performed by looking at phone bill records at the time of the accident. But according to the IIHS there is enough data to suggest that although hands-free phones eliminate the physical distraction of handling phones, the cognitive distraction still remains.

NHTSA's 2005 study on wireless phone interfaces showed that while participants had a tougher time steering with a hand held phone, it also made calls the fastest and had less dialing errors than a hands free unit. Our resistance to grasp this wireless technology may lead to slow adoption rates. Even in states or localities where cell phones are banned, there is a serious problem with compliance.

The IIHS's study adds that "... even if total compliance with bans on drivers' hand-held cell phone use can be achieved, crash risk will remain to the extent that drivers continue to use or switch to hands-free phones."

We agree that wireless technology is terrific, but just because it seems to be everywhere doesn't mean you have to use it everywhere. You never know: The most important call of your life could be the one you never make.

2

Cell Phone Use Is a Danger to Others

Mark Borgard

Mark Borgard worked as the night editor of the Wyoming Tribune-Eagle *before becoming editor of the* Kingman Daily Miner *in Kingman, Arizona.*

Multitasking and inconsiderateness are the two main reasons people use their cell phones while operating a car. Multitasking has become such a staple of modern life that people feel the need to multitask even when they are driving. Furthermore, in our society, where egotism and greed are valued, people only think about themselves and their own safety and tend to forget that they have a responsibility to keep others safe as well.

Kingman [Arizona] has a lot of bad drivers. Wait, let me rephrase that. I have no idea how well they can drive. Let's say, Kingman has a lot of drivers who demonstrate bad habits when they're behind the wheel. That's probably more accurate, though, the end result is the same: Get the H-e-double hockey sticks out of their way!

I used to think all those people driving erratically around here were on meth. I figured that if I could successfully get around them, I had saved a life . . . my own. Some looked the part: the beat-up pickup truck from the '70s; the car with dents all over it, maybe a smashed-in bumper, cracked windshield, one window broken out, something hanging from a bent antenna, obscene stickers plastered on the back. They might as well put a big sign on the car: "Police, please pull me over."

But this is 2010, and while many here may actually be on methamphetamines, most of the people I see anymore driving erratically have just one thing in common: a damn cell phone growing out of their ear. It never fails. When the idiot in front of me is moving too slow, cell phone. When I see a car weaving to one side, cell phone. When the pinhead decides to camp at the four-way stop, cell phone. It's become a game that makes me cringe when I play. How many morons on cell phones can I count on my way to work today?

As humans in the new millennium, we are expected to be able to multitask.

Breaking Bad Habits

I must admit, I've answered my cell from time to time while driving, but it's a habit I've forced myself to break. I figure any call will wait. You see, most (all) cell phones have this neat device which records the number of the caller, so you can call them back later, when you're not at the helm of a two-ton mostly metal motor vehicle. Or pull off into a parking lot. There's a bunch of them all over town.

I've come to the conclusion that two major forces are behind this problem. The first is the need to multitask. As humans in the new millennium, we are expected to be able to multitask. Heck, most of us would lose our jobs if we couldn't do 10 things at one time. Unfortunately, we've taken this "stay busy" desire with us when we get behind the wheel. At a time when we should be single-tasking—driving the damn car—we're conducting business, or talking with Aunt Helen, or yelling at our kids on the phone.

This phenomenon is nothing new, really. There's always been people who believe they can do 100 things while driving.

From putting on make-up, to scanning the morning paper, to stuffing their face with a burrito, it's a no-brainer for them. I've lived in big cities before, and the things you see during rush hour make you want to sell your car and buy a horse. The problem, however, has gotten worse as technology has improved.

An Inflated Sense of Self

The second is simple inconsideration. We just don't care about other people. Our lives are much more important than theirs. We're big shots. We drive big trucks, make a lot of money, live fascinating lives. We don't have time to pay attention to the road while we're driving. We figure that if we get in an accident, odds are our elite status, coupled with our financial security, will pretty much get us out of any scrape.

For others not so wealthy, they just don't care, period. They've been raised to care about themselves first, friends and family second, and pretty much no one else after that. They're the ones who are totally shocked when they crash into someone. Their first impulse is to flee, with no concern about whether someone may be hurt. If they're OK, then everything is peachy.

If you text while driving, you're an idiot. Your luck will run out eventually.

While the multitasking problem can be somewhat controlled by law enforcement, consideration for others is about impossible to teach when so many kids are ingrained with disrespect from the very beginning. I could write a book on what I think about the lack of parenting skills in our society, and it would sit on the shelf next to the thousands of other books on the subject. Unfortunately, we continue to accept this behavior as just a part of living in a "free" country. It's hogwash, certainly, but it's the bed we've made, so we are forced to sleep in it.

Running Out of Luck

I would love to buy a paint gun and tag the cars driven by people on cell phones, but I save that for my daydreams, because I would certainly end up in jail, or worse, cause the very accident I'm trying to avoid. No, I keep that "wish" to myself, in the same place where I keep the desire to buy a huge retractable mirror that I could raise on the back of my car when people come up on me with their high beams on. Maybe in my next life.

You may have noticed by now that I've said nothing about texting while driving. That is so stupid it doesn't deserve attention. If you text while driving, you're an idiot. Your luck will run out eventually. I just pray it doesn't run out when you're next to me on the road.

Prayer is definitely a task I'd gladly give up, at least while I'm driving. Drivers here, however, are bringing me closer to God every day.

3

Cell Phone Use While Driving May Not Always Pose a Danger

USA Today

USA Today is a national daily newspaper and has one of the widest circulations in the United States.

Whereas texting while driving is an indisputable safety hazard, data about drivers talking on their cell phones is less conclusive. Before lawmakers decide to introduce sweeping legislature to ban cell phone use in cars, more research is needed. States should not rely on anecdotal evidence when making decisions that will affect a majority of private and professional individuals.

Cellphones are as much a part of Americans' lives as cars these days. In fact, the nation now has more cellphone subscribers (270 million) than registered vehicles (254 million). The increasingly urgent questions are how dangerous it is to operate the two at the same time, and what to do about it.

The easiest call involves text messaging while driving. A study released this week [July 2009] by the Virginia Tech Transportation Institute confirms the obvious: Texting while driving is dumb and dangerous. Researchers found that truckers' collision risk was 23 times greater than when not texting. Fourteen states and the District of Columbia now ban text messaging for all drivers. What are the rest waiting for?

The far tougher question is whether drivers should be allowed to talk on their cellphones.

That's being debated state by state, and the current laws are a hodgepodge. No state bans all types of cellphone use for all drivers, but 21 states and the District of Columbia bar use by novice drivers. Five states (California, Connecticut, New Jersey, New York and Washington) plus D.C. prohibit the use of handheld cellphones while driving but allow hands-free devices.

Texting while driving is dumb and dangerous.

Looking for Hard Evidence

But lawmakers are setting policy more on the basis of tragic anecdotes than on hard data. The National Highway Traffic Safety Administration failed to publicly release statistics in 2003 that could have been a starting point. That outdated report, which finally became public last week, blamed 955 fatalities and 240,000 accidents on drivers using cellphones in 2002. Since then, 100 million more Americans have begun using cellphones, and far more than the 6% of drivers the study assumed are using them.

The NHTSA study also suggested that hands-free devices are no silver bullet, and a recent University of Utah study backed that up. Apparently, it's the conversation itself that distracts the driver's brain, not the type of device.

Solving the Problem

The growing unease about driving while using cellphones is creeping into national life. The bans on cellphone use by novice drivers and bus drivers (except in emergencies) make sense given the inexperience of young drivers and the responsibility of transit workers. But the National Safety Council and other safety advocates want to go further and impose a nationwide ban on all cellphone communication while driving. For a variety of reasons, that would be premature:

The Virginia Tech study suggests that cellphone talking and listening are only marginally riskier than non-distracted driving—and far less hazardous than tasks that require taking your eyes off the road.

In a vast nation, no one-size-fits-all solution seems appropriate.

Americans have become accustomed, if not addicted, to the convenience of being able to phone home to say where they are or ask what to pick up at the supermarket. Enforcement of a total ban would be a nightmare. Nearly a year after California outlawed talking on a handheld phone while driving, law enforcement statistics suggest motorists are having a hard time complying.

Drivers have a variety of in-car distractions: Talkative adults, unruly kids, navigation systems, Big Macs and Big Gulps. Where do you draw the line?

In a vast nation, no one-size-fits-all solution seems appropriate. Clearly, it's more dangerous to be yakking on a cellphone in a congested urban environment than on a wide-open rural interstate.

Cellphones have spread so quickly and widely that what's urgently needed is to begin collecting solid data on which to base sound policy. It should become mandatory to report real or suspected cellphone involvement in all accident reports. States should be required to collect those statistics, much as for alcohol-related accidents.

Perhaps, with time, data might prove that it is in the nation's best interest to enact broader curbs. First, though, it's important to get the facts and weigh the trade-offs.

4

Cell Phone Use Leads to "Inattention Blindness" and Can Prove Fatal

William Saletan

William Saletan is a national correspondent for Slate *and the author of the book* Bearing Right: How Conservatives Won the Abortion War.

When people talk on their phones while driving, their minds are blinded to what is going on around them, and they become safety hazards. While multitasking is often required on the job, surveys have shown that multitasking inside a car can have lethal consequences. When moving through the physical world at high speeds, it can be deadly to turn your mind to a phone conversation.

[In September 2008], 25 people died and 130 were injured in a train crash near Los Angeles. The cause, apparently, was a cell phone. In three hours of work before the crash, one of the engineers received 28 text messages and sent 29 more. He sent his last message 22 seconds before impact, just after passing a signal that would have alerted him to the disaster ahead.

Scientists call this phenomenon "cognitive capture" or "inattention blindness." The mind, captured by the world inside the phone, becomes blind to the world outside it. Millions of people move among us in this half-absent state. Mentally, they're living in another world. It's like the Rapture [the ascension of Christians into heaven during the end of the world], except that they've left their bodies behind.

Distracted People Are Everywhere

You see them everywhere. The woman alone in the grocery store, a bud in her ear, having an animated conversation with a wall of canned soup. The driver who drifts into your lane while counseling an invisible client. The jogger crossing four lanes of traffic, lost in her iPod. The dad who ignores his kids, living in his BlackBerry the way an alcoholic lives in a bottle.

The mind, captured by the world inside the phone, becomes blind to the world outside it.

In many ways, mobile phones are wonderful. Children can reach parents far away. Dissidents in dictatorships can get news and organize. Farmers in undeveloped countries can transact business. Through the phone, you can escape the confines of your environment.

The problem is that physically, you're still living in that environment. Like other creatures, you've evolved to function in the natural world, one setting at a time. Nature has never tested a species's ability to function in two worlds at once.

Now that test is underway. Half the world's people have mobile phones. Eighty-four percent of Americans have them. In this country, more than 2 billion text messages are exchanged per day. Wireless and entertainment companies are bringing television to handheld screens. Already, 40 million Americans use phones or other handheld devices to access the Internet, 27 million use them to watch video, and 19 million use them to download games. The world inside the phone becomes more vivid and engaging every day. It wants your ears, eyes, thumbs—all of you.

Mobile Devices Are Dangerous

That might be OK if you were standing still. But mobile devices have a habit of moving. In a survey this year by Nationwide Mutual Insurance, 81 percent of Americans admitted to talking on a cell phone while driving. Since 2001, in New York alone, more than 1 million tickets have been issued for holding phones at the wheel. In California, the rate is about 7,000 tickets per month. And that's just the people who get caught.

So how is this multitasking experiment going? Not so well. In the Nationwide survey, 45 percent of Americans said they've been hit or nearly hit by a driver on a cell phone. Studies show that the more tasks you dump on drivers—listening, evaluating, answering questions—the worse they perform. They drift off course, miss cues, overlook hazards, and react slowly. In brain scans, you can see the shift of blood flow from spatial-management to language-processing areas. It's the picture of a mind being sucked from one world into another.

Our performance on the two-worlds test, like all evolutionary experiments, can be measured in death. The Federal Railroad Administration reports seven cell-phone-related railway accidents in the last three years, five of them fatal. In California, Michigan, and Texas, police reports document annual cell-phone-related road accidents exceeding 1,000 per state. Six years ago, when only half of all Americans had cell phones, the Harvard Center for Risk Analysis linked them to 2,600 driving fatalities and 330,000 injuries per year. And that was before the texting boom.

Since 2001, in New York alone, more than 1 million tickets have been issued for holding phones at the wheel.

Navigating Two Worlds

Today, we're so enslaved to mobile devices that we rely on them even to translate the physical world. Misled by Global

Positioning System devices, people are driving cars into rivers, trees, and sand piles. Twice this year in Bedford Hills, N.Y., drivers have caused train crashes by steering onto the track because their GPS mistook it for a road. Warning signs, pavement markings, and reflective train-signal masts failed to stop them. They trusted the dashboard, not the windshield.

The real danger comes from being mentally sucked out of your world while operating thousands of pounds of metal at high speed.

If we don't want this two-worlds experiment to be regulated nature's way—by killing people—then we'd better regulate it ourselves. Here are a few proposed rules of the road. Multitasking is a glorious gift. We can't ban it, nor should we. Want to phone your spouse or your office while walking? Fine. The only life at stake is yours. Want to turn on your car radio or music player? Fine. Listening is easier than talking, and you can mentally or physically shut it off when necessary. Want to chat with your passenger? Fine again. Studies indicate that passenger conversations are less distracting than phone calls, apparently because you're sharing and often referring to the same environment.

The real danger comes from being mentally sucked out of your world while operating thousands of pounds of metal at high speed. Only five states prohibit driving while holding a phone, and if you're an adult with a hands-free phone, no legislator is even proposing to mess with you. That has to change, because research shows that even with a hands-free device, talking on a phone can impair driving skills more than intoxication does. If you need to talk to your spouse or boss, go right ahead—but first, pull over. You're free to visit the other world. Just don't leave your car moving in this one.

5

Cell Phone Use While Driving Can Make Women Safer

Bruce Siceloff

Bruce Siceloff is a reporter and editor at the News and Observer *in Raleigh, North Carolina.*

Although cell phone use while driving has come under intense scrutiny and is being banned by a growing number of states, many women feel that a cell phone used cautiously while driving can enhance their safety. Getting directions over the phone can be less distracting than scanning street signs and blocking traffic, and in remote or unsafe areas and situations, a cell phone can be a lifeline, connecting women to family, colleagues, or the police.

You think it's risky to phone while you drive? Gilda A. Branch feels safer when she's driving with her phone—and using it when she needs it.

"I can't tell you the countless times that my cell phone has probably saved my life," said Branch, 57, a real estate broker who lives in North Raleigh. "Sometimes it really is my lifeline."

Stopping the car to take a call isn't always a smart choice, she says. She might be in heavy traffic, or on a dark street where she doesn't feel comfortable.

When she's about to meet a client at a home she never visited before, she'll phone folks at her office to let them know

Bruce Siceloff, "They Call from the Car, Carefully," *News and Observer*, January 19, 2010. Reprinted by permission of The News & Observer of Raleigh, NC.

she got there OK. In an unfamiliar neighborhood, she might need to call her husband for navigation aid.

She would rather seek clear directions on her phone than be utterly confused as she drives down the street.

"It's less of a distraction to me than 'Oh my God, which way do I go at this intersection?'" Branch said.

She worries that highway safety crusaders will make her life harder with a ban on in-car phoning.

So does Susan Jancuski of Holly Springs, but for different reasons.

She would rather seek clear directions on her phone than be utterly confused as she drives down the street.

Calling from the Car Can Save Lives

Like Branch, Jancuski contends that tuning a radio can distract a driver more than talking on the phone.

Both women offer insights into the appeal of phoning while driving and the challenge of doing it safely.

Shuttling between her demanding job as a network engineer and her hectic duties as a single mother, Jancuski uses the phone while she drives to keep in touch with friends and family.

"It's making use of my free time, basically," said Jancuski, 46.

"It might be the only time I get to say 'Hi' to my grandmother. I'm so busy at work. And once I get home, I'm cooking, I'm doing the dishes."

Jancuski says many drivers aren't careful when they juggle telephones and other potentially dangerous distractions. She makes it a point to stay focused on the road and the traffic around her, even when she's on the phone.

"I am watching my mirrors all the time, too," Jancuski said. "I'm very good at this. I'm a mom with two children. We are trained to do this."

Learning from Mistakes

She sends text messages only when stopped at a red light. (And now that texting is illegal, she says she does it only "rarely.")

She takes multitasking seriously.

She'll drop her phone in mid-conversation if traffic gets intense or an ambulance shows up in her rear-view mirror. She turns down the radio for a conversation with her children, and she stops the car if the talk gets heated.

She takes multitasking seriously. She learned her lesson at age 16, when she looked away from the road to wave to a friend—and sideswiped another car.

"That taught me to always pay attention. I know I can make that mistake," Jancuski said. "And so I'm very careful."

6

Cell Phone Use While Driving Needs Stiff Penalties

Ian Mulgrew

Ian Mulgrew is a Canadian journalist and author who writes a legal-affairs column for the Vancouver Sun. *He has written and cowritten several books, among them* Who Killed Cindy James? *and* Amazon Extreme.

In the face of skyrocketing vehicle crashes caused by drivers' cell phone use, it is time that lawmakers introduce severe punishments for using electronic devices while operating a vehicle. In order to curb talking and texting while driving, drivers should face mandatory prison terms if they cause serious harm or fatalities.

If the provincial Liberals are going to jump on the distracted-driving bandwagon, is a $167 ticket for using a cellphone or texting while driving punishment enough?

Don't we also need overt criminal sanctions?

In Britain, they've gotten so serious about distracted drivers that judges have been told prolonged texting should be considered as serious an aggravating factor in sentencing as impaired driving or street racing.

You don't even have to be texting at the time of an accident—a woman was convicted because the ping of arriving e-mail was thought enough to distract her so that she plowed into a parked car, killing another woman.

She got 21 months in prison under new British guidelines designed to fight distracted driving, though prosecutors quickly appealed, calling the sentence "unduly lenient."

The appeal court agreed the punishment was on the light end of the spectrum but declined to extend the sentence.

It did serve notice to the lower courts that such recklessness on the part of drivers should no longer be countenanced.

Legal Action Against Distracted Driving

Britain is leading the crusade against distracted driving.

A film by Gwent Police in Wales about the dangers of texting and driving that was posted on YouTube recently [2009] went viral. It features a 17-year-old girl being distracted while driving two friends in her car, precipitating a devastating and horrifying crash.

Utah passed a law threatening 15 years in prison for those who end up in an accident as a result of texting and driving.

Most European nations, 50 countries around the globe and more than a dozen American states have already responded to the increasing carnage and currently ban drivers from using hand-held cellphones or other devices.

President Barack Obama last month [October 2009] prohibited all federal employees (including postal workers and military personnel) from texting while driving whenever they are on the job driving a government vehicle.

Utah passed a law threatening 15 years in prison for those who end up in an accident as a result of texting and driving.

By comparison [British Columbian] Solicitor-General Kash Heed's provincial legislation—which should become law in January—seems tame with its paltry fine and three penalty points for drivers caught chatting, e-mailing, tweeting or texting while behind the wheel.

Even Ontario's new law means drivers who use their fingers to dial cellphones or send text messages will be liable for a fine of $500.

The death of a Victoria-area man in a two-vehicle crash last January underscored the need to address the problem locally.

Cellphone use is apparently the leading cause of accidents blamed on distracted driving—which are said to claim on average 117 lives a year in B.C. and to send 1,400 to hospital.

Seemingly, people yakking on cellphones while driving are four times more likely to crash, and texting is at least as dangerous: Nobody should be doing it.

Punishment Is Necessary

Six other provinces have similar laws in place, but Heed boasts that ours will be the most comprehensive—only hands-free cellphones and devices that require one touch to activate will be permitted.

The death of a Victoria-area man in a two-vehicle crash last January underscored the need to address the problem locally.

Saanich police say Michael Edward Wolsynuk, 26, was texting and lost control of his truck, which vaulted a concrete median and slammed head-on into an oncoming truck.

The B.C. Association of Chiefs of Police earlier this year urged a total ban on cellphone use by drivers, even with hands-free devices.

Heed didn't go that far and his proposals won't do the whole job.

Ottawa must get on board and judicial support is necessary.

I don't think anyone disagrees it's time for stiff punishments and prison time when texting or utilizing electronic devices is a factor in a crash—especially when serious injury or death is involved.

7

Real Estate Agents Need to Use Their Cell Phones While Driving

Jordan Wyner

When this article appeared, Jordan Wyner was a student reporter for the Columbia Missourian, *a newspaper published by the Missouri School of Journalism.*

The state of Missouri is trying to outlaw the use of cell phones while driving, but real estate agents are opposing the measure. For them, a cell phone is an integral part of their profession and an absolute necessity. They argue that they have to make and answer calls while in their cars and that any restrictions on cell phone use in cars will result in either lost business or a slide into criminality.

In the past three years, the Missouri legislature has attempted six times to pass some kind of legislation limiting drivers' use of a cell phone. Three bills would have banned talking on a hand-held cell phone in the car, and the other three would have banned texting.

All of them failed.

Rep. Scott Lipke, R-Jackson, broke the barrier in the legislature's last session. He introduced an omnibus crime bill—passed and signed by Gov. Jay Nixon on July 9 [2009]— that makes sending, reading and writing text messages while driving against the law for people 21 and younger.

Rep. Joe Smith, R-St. Charles, whose own attempts to push through legislation limiting hand-held cell phone use failed, said he thinks the new law slipped through without the usual opposition because it only applies to people 21 and younger.

Sen. Ryan McKenna, D-Crystal City, who introduced his own bill this session limiting text messaging while driving, said, "the house was uncomfortable with the bill without the age restriction."

It's not the telecommunication lobby, as one might think, that wants to beat back efforts to limit cell phone use.

Cell phone legislation, such as McKenna and Smith's bills, usually runs up against some powerful opposition: legislators who see the limitations as an invasion of privacy and real estate lobbyists.

Real Estate Lobbyists Strike Back

Yes, real estate lobbyists. It's not the telecommunication lobby, as one might think, that wants to beat back efforts to limit cell phone use. In fact, the telecommunications companies "helped write legislation so it fit Missouri statutes," Smith said. "They did a lot of clarifying. They didn't do anything to harm it."

The real opposition was seen from lobbyists representing real estate agents, who often use their cars as traveling offices.

"My office is the city of Columbia," ReMax realtor Brent Gardner said. "My job is a little different than most people in that I'm mobile."

The Missouri Association of Realtors takes the following position: "We're generally opposed to restrictions on cell phone use, when they're used as cell phones" said Sam Licklider, a lobbyist for the association. "The simple fact is, (realtors) are in their car a lot and they use their phones for business." Lick-lider said his association has not yet taken an official stand on text messaging while driving.

Legal Wrangling

While Smith's latest bill addressing hand-held cell phone limitations stalled in the House Public Safety Committee, McKenna's bill addressed text messaging in the car and passed in the senate with a vote of 31-3. The bill then also stalled in the House Public Safety Committee.

When asked about McKenna's bill, one of the three dissenting voters, Sen. Jason Crowell, R-Cape Girardeau, said that there was already a law in place to cover text messaging in the car. The law, nicknamed the Careless & Imprudent Driving law, is an umbrella law that covers dangerous behaviors in the car, Crowell said. The other two senators did not return calls for comment.

You can't legislate stupidity.

The three dissenting voters for McKenna's 2009 bill—Crowell, Chuck Purgason, R-Caulfield, and Jolie Justus, D-Jackson County—have received $18,075, $3,300, and $1,950 respectively in campaign contributions from real estate lobbyists.

Crowell said lobbyists did not influence his vote.

"We currently have a statewide catch-all with the (careless and imprudent law)," he said. "I am opposed to texting but if we go down this route, we're going to have to pass a law for every behavior that is not wise to do while driving."

Crowell listed activities that he felt were as dangerous as texting in the car, citing eating, reading, applying makeup and changing clothes.

"I actually saw somebody reading the newspaper while driving," he said.

Crowell thinks texting while driving needs to be stopped, but the careless and imprudent law should be "beefed-up" instead of adding a separate law banning texting.

Legislating Stupidity

A professor of criminology at the University of Missouri-St. Louis, Finn-Aage Esbensen, takes a similar view.

"You can't legislate stupidity," he said. "We already have umbrella laws that address the issue. There really is no need (for a specific texting law)."

Esbensen said a texting law would be unrealistic to enforce and unlikely to deter texting drivers.

"Public education and informal social control by others are more likely to work," he said.

On the other hand, Sgt. Shelley Jones, Columbia Police Department Traffic Unit supervisor, thinks legislation banning texting while driving is a good idea.

"I think texting while driving is excessively dangerous, so I think it would be beneficial," she said. Under the Careless and Imprudent law, "if they're driving down the street and texting and they're not committing any traffic violations, I don't have reasonable suspicion to pull them over," she said.

Starting Aug. 28 [2009], Jones and her traffic unit will be able to pull over anyone 21 or under that they see texting in the car.

Although they said the under-21 law is a step in the right direction, McKenna and Smith aren't done yet.

"A lot of the time in Jefferson City, you have to crawl before you can walk," McKenna said. Of a bill applying to all ages, he said, "I plan on proposing it again next year."

"You're basically inviting people to come to Missouri and text while driving, unless they're 21 or under," Smith said. He plans to continue fighting for all-age legislation as well.

For now, Gardner and other Missouri real estate agents can continue to use their phones as they please, provided they are over the age of 21.

8

Hands-Free Devices
Keep Drivers Safe

Canwest News Service

Canwest News Service is a Canadian commercial news network, covering a range of content areas from breaking news to in-depth analysis.

To avoid distracted-driving accidents, drivers should invest in new technologies, such as hands-free and Bluetooth devices, that allow them to keep their eyes on the road and avoid crashes. The public needs to be educated about the grave dangers of using a cell phone while driving, and individuals need to take steps to keep themselves and other drivers safe.

Ontario Provincial Police Sgt. Pierre Chamberland remembers the incident well. A young mother was driving home in the Holland Marsh area north of Toronto. Distracted by the cellphone conversation she was having with her mother, she veered off the road into the adjacent canal and was killed.

"There have been a good many very serious accidents because drivers were distracted. Cellphones and BlackBerrys are among the chief distractions," he says.

Chief distractions yes; the only distractions, no. Almost anyone who drives regularly has a horror story to tell.

Marc Choma, director of communications for the Canadian Wireless Telecommunications Association [CWTA] in Ottawa, says he regularly passes a driver who reads his news-

Canwest News Service, "Clearing the Air for Safe Driving; Hands-Free Only," Kelowna .com, December 8, 2009. Reproduced by permission.

paper spread out on the steering wheel. In another instance, he saw a woman with five children in a mini-van reading to them to entertain them as she drove.

"You see lots of foolish stuff every day," he says. "The challenge is coming up with laws and regulations that can be enforced."

Legislation and Safe-Driving Education

Canada's provinces seem to be doing just that when it comes to electronic devices such as wireless phones.

Only Alberta and Nova Scotia remain holdouts when it comes to passing or planning to pass distracted-driving legislation, Mr. Choma says. Like police forces, the wireless communication industry welcomes the move, he adds.

Investing in that Blue Tooth earpiece or visor-mounted adaptor can and does save lives and injuries.

"We have always believed when it comes to driving there should always be two hands on the wheel and two eyes on the road," he says.

To back its safe-driving beliefs, the CWTA and its members—wireless service providers such as Rogers, Bell Canada and Telus—have created safe-driving education campaigns. The latest is Focus on Driving, a series of tips and rules to follow, accessed through the www.CWTA.ca website. "Our view is that people seldom need to make or receive calls when driving, and they never need to email," he says. "But if a call is essential, all our members now offer affordable hands-free attachments for most wireless devices."

Investing in that Blue Tooth earpiece or visor-mounted adaptor can and does save lives and injuries, he says.

Encourage Use of Hands-Free Devices

Rogers Wireless is such a firm believer in safe driving that it has made available discounted hands-free Blue Tooth devices to all its 30,000 employees across Canada, says Reade Barber, director of data product management.

"We also educate them to make, or respond to, only absolutely necessary calls when driving, and never text, message or email," he says.

I have loaded all the numbers I call regularly into the memory, so all I have to do is press the button then say call followed by the person's name.

All of Rogers' current wireless phone offerings are now Blue Tooth-equipped, he says.

"I use a visor-mounted device that sends calls through the speakers in my car," he says. "My BlackBerry is also equipped with voice controls. I mount it on the dashboard and to receive or make a call. I just press one button and then give a voice prompt.

"I have loaded all the numbers I call regularly into the memory, so all I have to do is press the button then say call followed by the person's name. If I want the incoming call to go to voice mail, I just say 'ignore.'"

Blue Tooth devices are widely available in Canada, says Jennifer Cauble, director of marketing for Blue Ant Wireless Corp. of Santa Monica, Calif., a leading Blue Tooth manufacturer. In Canada, the company sells through major chains such as Future Shop and Best Buy and through many of the wireless companies' own stores.

"Canadians seem to prefer visor-mounted devices over Blue Tooth earphones, and there is always a sharp jump in sales in the days leading up to and immediately following new legislation governing driving and cellphone use," she says.

That means look for a rush to electronics and wireless stores in British Columbia in the days before and after Jan. 1 [2010], when that province's distracted-driving legislation comes into force, and in Newfoundland and Prince Edward Island some time in 2010.

In Ontario, the rush came in the days leading up to Oct. 26 [2009] and immediately afterward. That is when the province got its controlling distracted driving and promoting green transportation law.

Until Feb. 1 [2010], the penalty for using hand-controlled electronic devices while driving is a court summons and, on conviction, a $500 fine, Sgt. Chamberland says. On Feb. 1, the province will introduce new distracted driving tickets; the fine will be about $125, he says.

"Police officers can use their discretion as to whether to issue a summons or ticket, like with many other traffic offences," he says. "The worst offenders will get the summonses."

As of the beginning of this month [December 2009] OPP officers had issued 22 summonses and 1,109 warnings, Sgt. Chamberland says.

"We have indeed been laying charges but mostly in the worst-case situations. Right now, we are focused on educating the public."

9

Hands-Free Devices Will Not Make Drivers Safer

Melissa Healy

Melissa Healy is a Los Angeles Times *staff writer.*

Despite a push by technology companies to portray hands-free mobile phone devices as safe for drivers, phone conversations in the car are still a major distraction and a significant cause of traffic accidents. According to recent research, the type of phone or mobile device and even the type of conversation had while driving is statistically irrelevant. Only technologies that lock phones once the vehicle starts moving—or shut off cell phones while driving—are effective ways to prevent crash fatalities.

You know the shot: Seen from above, the hero (or villain) is hurtling down the freeway, top down, one hand on the wheel and the other clutching a cellphone to his ear. It's Hollywood's image of how deals are made, dates are broken and gossip is shared, at 65 miles per hour.

On Tuesday [July 1, 2008], that shot will be history. California motorists—as well as those in Washington state, where a similar law was recently passed—will be prohibited from talking on hand-held cellular phones while driving. Most, however, will likely continue their wireless business using headsets, speakers or other hands-free devices.

[California] Gov. Arnold Schwarzenegger says the new law will reduce accidents. "Getting people's hands off their phones and onto their steering wheels will save lives and make California's roads safer," he said earlier this month [June 2008].

That, however, is not what the research finds. Scientists says that when mixing cellphones and driving, the number of hands available for the tasks is not the limiting factor.

Instead, it's a driver's attention and processing capacity. These are often stretched beyond safe limits when someone juggles the complex tasks of negotiating traffic and conversing with another remotely.

Worse than Being Drunk

"There are limits to how much we can multi-task, and that combination of cellphone and driving exceeds the limits," says David Strayer, a University of Utah psychologist who has found that by many measures, drivers yakking on cellphones are more dangerous behind the wheel than those who are drunk, whether the conversation is carried on by handset *or* headset.

Scientists say that when mixing cellphones and driving, the number of hands available for the tasks is not the limiting factor.

In a 2005 study, published in the journal *Human Factors*, Strayer put 41 adult drivers through four sessions in a simulator, re-creating realistic driving conditions along a 24-mile stretch of freeway.

Over three days, the subjects took the wheel in various ways: sober and off-the-phone; legally under the influence of orange-juice-and-vodka cocktails; while talking with a research assistant by hand-held cellphone; and chatting over a hands-free cellphone device. The result: Compared with drivers exceeding the legal blood alcohol limit, users of cellphones—hand-held or hands-free—reacted 18% more slowly to braking by the car in front and were more likely to get in a rear-end collision.

What's more, the talkers seemed to compensate for their slowed response time by falling farther behind the car in front—a pattern likely to slow traffic and exacerbate congestion.

"And you don't get any better with practice," Strayer adds. In his lab, subjects who reported they use a cellphone a lot when driving "show every bit as much impairment" than those who do so infrequently.

Although no studies looked at the safety of cellphone chatter by drivers of manual-transmission cars, Strayer acknowledged that stick-shifters may reap immediate safety improvements by switching to a hands-free device for cellphone calls. But he cautions that, in principle, that would merely bring these motorists up to "the same level of impairment" as automatic-transmission drivers talking on cellphones.

He says cellphone bans that exempt hands-free devices "are half-measures that aren't really taking into account the available scientific evidence. And it's not just one source of evidence," he adds; in recent years, dozens of studies, using a wide range of methods, have concluded there is no difference between driving performance of people using hand-held phones and hands-free devices.

Negative Effects of Talking While Driving

For instance, in a 2005 Australian study published in the *British Medical Journal*, researchers interviewed, during a 27-month period, 456 hospitalized cellphone users who had each been involved in a crash. The scientists combed the drivers' call records to see how cellphone use affected their driving. Whether they talked hands-free or with a phone clasped to their ear, the result was the same: During calls, and for 10 minutes after their completion, a driver's likelihood of crashing shot up fourfold.

In the lab, multi-tasking drivers fare little better. A recent study showed powerfully how doing two seemingly simple tasks can overload the brain and cause errors of judgment.

Marcel Just, a neuroscientist at Carnegie Mellon University in Pittsburgh, conducted brain imaging of 29 young adults to gauge the cognitive demands of simultaneously driving and listening. Lying in a functional magnetic resonance imaging machine, the subjects steered a simulated car down a winding road. On a second run, they steered the car while listening to general-knowledge statements and identifying them as true or false.

The study, published in April [2008] in the journal *Brain Research*, found that subjects who were allowed to navigate undisturbed showed robust activity in the brain's parietal lobe, a region long associated with spatial sense, distance calculations and judgments that require a person to calculate his whereabouts in a broader physical environment. When the task of listening to the sentences was added, blood flowed to different parts of the brain generally involved in the processing of language. As those language areas came alive, activity in the parietal lobe declined by almost 40%.

A recent study showed powerfully how doing two seemingly simple tasks can overload the brain and cause errors of judgment.

Failing to Drive Safely

While engaged in the listening task, drivers simultaneously listening to sentences veered off the road and onto the shoulder almost 50% more often than those allowed to focus uniquely on driving. And all they had to do was steer the car forward:

no cars veered into their lane, no children darted into the road, no construction site loomed up unexpectedly.

"Before we ever ran any of these studies, some thought, 'Well, these were two independent tasks, performed by two independent brain areas,'" Just says. But certain brain regions are very likely critical to both tasks, he adds, and the flow of traffic in the multi-tasking brain appears to have slowed as a result. "It can only do so much at a time."

Listening Isn't So Easy

People mistakenly believe that listening is a light burden and readily adjustable when competing demands crop up, Just says. But he believes that spoken language is neither simple to process nor easy to tune out.

"For a driver, it's insidious," he says. "You think driving is kind of effortless, chatting is kind of effortless, so what the heck. And you can combine them and, mostly, you're fine. But in hard driving, that can be a definite risk."

If listening is demanding, talking appears to be even harder, especially when the other person isn't in the car. In a study published in June [2008] in the journal *Experimental Psychology*, University of South Carolina psychologist Amit Almor put 47 subjects in a surround-sound console and had them detect visual shapes on a monitor or use a mouse to track a moving target on a screen.

When the subjects listened to prerecorded narratives, their attention to the visual task before them dipped significantly. But as they then answered questions about what they'd seen, or even just got ready to speak, their attention to the task on the screen didn't dip—it plummeted.

"It has not anything to do with manipulating the phone or holding it," Almor says. "It's the attentional demands of conversation that matters." Those demands shoot up, he adds, when drivers expect to contribute to conversations.

More Distractions on the Horizon

Some researchers, in fact, fear that the new law may cause more traffic accidents, not fewer, because they envision more distractions for many motorists. When ring tones chime and drivers scramble to find their newly purchased headsets—or, alternatively, scan the roadsides for police enforcing the new ban—their attention, already stretched, will be further taxed.

Strayer suggests, too, that motorists who believe they're now safer because they're not using a hand-held may now spend more time on the phone in the belief that cellphones' safety issues have been addressed.

If listening is demanding, talking appears to be even harder, especially when the other person isn't in the car.

It's clear many drivers agree with Schwarzenegger's contention that the roads will be safer. Denise Spooner of Claremont says that although she has her doubts about other drivers, she's pretty sure that hands-free-calling-while-driving has made her a less-hazardous motorist. A stick-shift owner—and a longtime user of headsets—Spooner, a 52-year-old historian at Cal State Fullerton, says having both hands available for rapid response "makes the difference."

"What else," she asks, "could it be?"

10

Smartphone Applications Designed to Curb Cell Phone Use Are Imperfect

Peter Svensson

Peter Svensson is a technology writer for the Associated Press.

To prevent tragic car accidents, technology companies now offer electronic devices that block drivers' phones while the vehicle is in motion. Parents can install the device on their teenagers' phones to insure that they don't text or make calls while driving a car or riding with their friends. However, override functions and the costs of the new technologies might curb their usefulness. If the industry does not develop a clear plan for overcoming distracted driving, the problem might only be exacerbated.

Cars use lights, bells and buzzers to remind drivers to fasten their seat belts as they start their engines.

It would seem natural, then, to offer motorists friendly, yet stern warnings about another bad habit: holding a cell phone while driving, whether for texting or talking.

Several software and gadget companies—many of them at the country's biggest trade show for the wireless industry last week in Las Vegas—have sprung up to address that challenge. But creating an effective, widespread solution looks a lot harder than putting in reminders for seat belts.

Peter Svensson, "Apps to Curb Texting While Driving Have Tough Task," *Yahoo! News/ Associated Press*, March 28, 2010. Reproduced by permission.

Furthermore, we're only just beginning to figure out what constitutes a dangerous distraction, and how best to curb it. Are handsfree conversations dangerous? What about dictating text messages to your phone? Does everyone need help staying away from the phone while driving, or just teens and employees?

Many states ban drivers from using cell phones without handsfree devices, but a recent insurance industry study found that such laws haven't reduced crashes. It's not clear why, but one reason might be that drivers flout the laws.

At least a dozen startups have produced phone applications designed to curb the temptation to use the phone while driving.

Many states ban drivers from using cell phones without handsfree devices, but a recent insurance industry study found that such laws haven't reduced crashes.

But these applications work only on some phones and have a hard time figuring out if the user is actually driving. Potentially important players—wireless carriers, cell phone makers, auto manufacturers and the federal government— have yet to step in, leaving the field to smaller companies that lack the clout to put services in widespread use.

And some of the tools might not even improve safety.

"Technology without a clear vision for how it's going to actually help drivers could end up doing more harm than good," said John Lee, professor of industrial and systems engineering at the University of Wisconsin in Madison.

For instance, Drive Safely Corp. proposes to put software on phones to detect, using a built-in GPS chip, when a device is moving faster than 15 miles per hour. To figure out whether the phone is being used by a driver or a passenger, who can safely text in the car, Drive Safely intends to have the phone flash a series of numbers and letters that the user has to match on the keypad. The assumption is that drivers won't be able to match the sequence while watching the road, so they won't be able to unlock it for texting.

Lee suspects that won't deter teens, and perhaps other motorists, from trying.

"They will try to do that task while they drive," Lee said. "And by making that task really difficult, you make it more dangerous for them."

Technology without a clear vision for how it's going to actually help drivers could end up doing more harm than good.

A half-dozen other services are either available or in the works to use the phone's GPS chip to figure out if the device is moving. With names such as ZoomSafer, TxtBlocker, Cell-Safety and Textecution, these software tools can respond in a number of ways, such as holding incoming text messages in quarantine until after the trip or by blocking the writing of new ones.

They're expensive compared with regular downloadable applications, possibly because the startups figure that parents of teens will pay for a feeling of security. Some cost $40 to buy, then charge recurring fees of $4 or so per month.

None of them can tell, however, whether the owner is in a bus or a train rather than an automobile, or if someone in a car is just a passenger and not the driver. So most of these tools have an override option—which a determined motorist can take advantage of even while driving.

Power consumption from constant GPS use is also a concern, possibly draining the battery twice as fast on some phones and applications.

Another approach is to dispense with using the GPS chip and rely on the car to tell the phone that it's in a moving car.

Services such as Cellcontrol and Key2SafeDriving come with a small gadget that plugs in to a port generally found under the car's steering column. It's intended to help mechanics diagnose problems with the car, but it can also tell the gadget how fast the car is moving. If it's above a certain speed, a wireless signal is sent to the phone's Bluetooth receiver. The application then goes into "drive mode," locking out some features.

This method avoids the battery drain of GPS. But it adds the element of hardware installation, and the cost of the Bluetooth transmitter. If the phone isn't set up to use a particular transmitter, the software doesn't work. That assures that you can pair your phone with a particular vehicle, but it means you'll have to remember to turn off the phone when you're borrowing a car.

A problem common to both GPS and Bluetooth approaches is that the applications will only run on certain phones. The phones most commonly supported by the distracted-driving apps are BlackBerrys, high-end Nokia phones and devices running Microsoft Corp.'s Windows Mobile or Google Inc.'s Android software.

Phones that lack "smart" operating systems are out of luck, as is Apple Inc.'s iPhone. Apple doesn't allow third-party software to run "in the background," so it can't figure out if the iPhone is in a moving car.

It's questionable whether replacing manual manipulation of the phone with voice commands is safer.

"It's going to be expensive for companies like our own to continually try to catch up with the multitude of phones," said Joe Brennan at Trinity-Noble, which has a GPS-based app called Guardian Angel MP.

Brennan believes the only viable long-term solution is to install a radio jammer that blocks all communication between the driver's phone and the outside world. The company has been developing such a jammer for years, but it's illegal in the United States. Brennan says its effect is so specific that passengers can still use their phones.

Lee believes that eventually, some sort of solution will be built into cars and take advantage of their electronics, displays and controls to reduce phone distractions. Ford Motor Co.'s optional Sync system already links cell phones to the car's controls, reads out text messages and understands spoken commands.

It's questionable whether replacing manual manipulation of the phone with voice commands is safer though. Research has shown that cell phone conversations are distracting to drivers whether they're holding the phone or using a hands-free system.

The Department of Transportation's Research and Innovative Technology Administration is looking at ways to reduce phone distractions, but it wants to make sure that technology promising better safety won't also create an additional distraction.

Peter Appel, the agency's head, warned against waiting for technology to solve what's really a problem of behavior: "The real challenge that we face is: How do you get drivers to just drive?"

11

Cell Phone Users Cause Traffic Delays

University of Utah News

Contrary to popular belief, hands-free cell phones are just as un-safe as regular cell phones. Talking on the phone while driving slows drivers' reaction time as much as having an unlawful blood alcohol level does. But apart from endangering themselves and others by swerving and ignoring traffic signals, distracted drivers also slow down traffic. Even small delays on route to work or school add up over time and cost Americans many millions of dollars every year.

Motorists who talk on cell phones drive slower on the freeway, pass sluggish vehicles less often and take longer to complete their trips, according to a University of Utah study that suggests drivers on cell phones congest traffic.

"At the end of the day, the average person's commute is longer because of that person who is on the cell phone right in front of them," says University of Utah psychology Professor Dave Strayer, leader of the research team. "That SOB on the cell phone is slowing you down and making you late."

"If you talk on the phone while you're driving, it's going to take you longer to get from point A to point B, and it's going to slow down everybody else on the road," says Joel Cooper, a doctoral student in psychology.

Cooper is scheduled to present the study in Washington on Wednesday, Jan. 16 [2008] during the Transportation Research Board's annual meeting. The board is part of the National Academies, parent organization of the National Academy of Sciences, National Academy of Engineering and Institute of Medicine.

Cooper and Strayer conducted the study with Ivana Vladisavljevic, a doctoral student in civil and environmental engineering, and Peter Martin, an associate professor of civil and environmental engineering and director of the University of Utah Traffic Lab.

When young adults talk on cell phones while driving, their reaction times become as slow as reaction times for senior citizens.

Martin says that, combined with Strayer's previous research, the new study shows "cell phones not only make driving dangerous, they cause delay too."

Previous Research on Wireless Phones and Driving

In recent years, Strayer's research group has published studies showing that:

• Hands-free cell phones are no less dangerous while driving than hand-held cell phones because the conversation itself is the major distraction.

• When young adults talk on cell phones while driving, their reaction times become as slow as reaction times for senior citizens.

• Drivers talking on cell phones are as impaired as drivers with the 0.08 percent blood alcohol level that defines drunken driving in most states.

Highway statistics suggest drivers on cell phones are four times more likely to be in an accident, and Strayer's earlier research suggests the risk is 5.36 times greater.

The Cellular Telecommunications and Internet Association claims 240 million U.S. subscribers in a nation of 303 million people. An insurance company survey estimated 73 percent of wireless users talk while driving. Another survey found that during any given daytime moment, 10 percent of U.S. drivers are using cellular phones.

The researchers note that 50 countries have adopted laws banning handheld phones while driving. But they say hands-free phone conversations are distracting, "thus, the majority of current regulation appears to be misguided."

How the New Study Was Conducted

The earlier studies found that cell phone users follow at greater distances, are slower to hit the brakes and are slower to regain speed after braking. But such research didn't examine how traffic efficiency is influenced by individual cell phone users.

That led to Strayer and Martin discussing the possibility of using computers to simulate numerous individual cell phone users' driving behavior and thus overall traffic. So their doctoral students—Cooper and Vladisavljevic—conducted the new study as a step toward an eventual computer "microsimulation" of numerous drivers and vehicles.

The new study used a PatrolSim driving simulator. A person sits in a front seat equipped with gas pedal, brakes, steering and displays from a Ford Crown Victoria patrol car. Realistic traffic scenes are projected on three screens around the driver.

Designing the Study

The new study involved 36 University of Utah psychology undergraduates. Each student drove through six, 9.2-mile-long freeway scenarios, two each in low, medium and high density traffic, corresponding to freeway speeds of 70 mph to 40 mph. Each 9.2-mile drive included 3.9 miles with two lanes in each direction and 5.3 miles with three lanes each way. Traffic speed and flow mimicked Interstate 15 in Salt Lake City.

Each student spoke on a hands-free cell phone during one drive at each level of traffic density, and did not use a cell phone during the other three drives. A volunteer on the other end of the phone was told to maintain a constant exchange of conversation.

The drivers were told to obey the 65-mph speed limit, and use turn signals. That let participants decide their own speeds, following distances and lane changes.

"We designed the study so that traffic would periodically slow in one lane and the other lane would periodically free up," Cooper says. "It created a situation where progress down the road was clearly impeded by slower moving vehicles, and a driver would benefit by moving to the faster lane, whether it was right or left."

[I]f you have a lot of people who are not changing lanes and driving slower, this could substantially reduce traffic flow.

Talking While Driving Means Plodding Along

"Results indicated that, when drivers conversed on a cell phone, they made fewer lane changes, had a lower overall mean speed and a significant increase in travel time in the medium and high density driving conditions," the researchers wrote.

• In medium and high density traffic, drivers talking on cell phones were 21 percent and 19 percent, respectively, less likely to change lanes (roughly six lane changes per 9.2-mile drive versus seven or eight lane changes by drivers not on cell phones).

That may seem minor, "but if you have a lot of people who are not changing lanes and driving slower, this could substantially reduce traffic flow," Cooper says.

When considered with the earlier studies, "it's going to increase traffic congestion," says Strayer. "You have motorists on cell phones who tend to drive slower, their reaction times are slower, if they do hit the brakes it takes them longer to come back up to highway speed, and they are less likely to change lanes. Overall, they are more likely to gum up the highways."

• In low, medium and high traffic density, cell phone users spent 31 percent, 16 percent and 12 percent, respectively, more time following within 200 feet of a slow lead vehicle than undistracted drivers. That meant they spent 25 to 50 more seconds following another vehicle during the 9.2-mile drive.

"If you were not distracted by talking on a cell phone, you would overtake and pass the slower vehicle and come to your destination faster," Vladisavljevic says.

Compared with undistracted motorists, drivers on cell phones drove an average of 2 mph slower and took 15 to 19 seconds longer to complete the 9.2 miles.

Strayer adds: "If you get two or three people gumming up the system, it starts to cascade and slows everybody's commute."

He acknowledges that, "in itself, staying in a lane and not passing might be construed as being safer, just as driving slightly slower or having a greater following distance also could be considered safer. But if you are doing that so you can take your mind off the road and talk on the phone, that isn't safer."

• Compared with undistracted motorists, drivers on cell phones drove an average of 2 mph slower and took 15 to 19 seconds longer to complete the 9.2 miles. That may not seem like much, but is likely to be compounded if 10 percent of all drivers are talking on wireless phones at the same time, Cooper says.

Delays Are Increasing

Vladisavljevic already has begun computer "microsimulations" of multiple vehicles. She tried the simulation repeatedly with the proportion of drivers on cell phones ranging from none to 25 percent.

"We saw an increase in delays for all cars in a system, and the delays increased as the percentage of drivers on cell phones increased," she says.

Strayer says it is important to show how cell phone use affects traffic because "when people have tried to do cost-benefit analyses to decide whether we should regulate cell phones, they often don't factor in the cost to society associated with increased commute times, excess fuel used by stop-and-go traffic and increased air pollution, as well as hazards associated with drivers distracted by cell phone conversations."

Martin says transportation analysts include two components—accidents and delay—when they calculate the "user costs" associated with road travel.

"A fatal accident could cost as much as $5 million when we take into account medical, property and loss-of-income costs," says Martin. "Delay is measured by a composite number representing a measure of the value of a typical American traveler's time. Today, this number is about $13 per hour. While the costs associated with accidents seem high, there are so very few of them, comparatively, they actually are dwarfed by the user costs associated with delay. If we compile the millions of drivers distracted by cell phones and their small delays, and convert them to dollars, the costs are likely to be dramatic. Cell phones cost us dearly."

12

Texting While Driving Is More Dangerous than Driving Under the Influence

Charles Moore

Charles Moore is news editor for the web site Low End Mac and the author of its Miscellaneous Ramblings column, which he has been writing for more than ten years.

Cell phones have infiltrated every aspect of our private and public lives, and schools have to either ban or jam students' cell phones to guarantee a distraction-free learning environment. Studies have shown that drivers—especially teenagers—who talk or text while operating a vehicle are as distracted and impaired as drunk drivers. Any use of mobile phones in cars is hazardous, but texting produces an effect equivalent to high blood-alcohol levels. Worse, unlike drunk drivers, who might be aware of their impairment and act accordingly, texting drivers are oblivious to the risk they are taking.

For someone who derives part of his living from writing about smartphones, I'm paradoxically something of a cell-phone curmudgeon—indeed, a just plain telephone curmudgeon. I appreciate the utilitarian value of telephony and related technologies, but I strenuously resist the premise that being reachable by phone 24/7 wherever one might happen to be is a good or desirable thing.

100 years ago acerbic lexicographer and self-styled cynic Ambrose Bierce dismissed the telephone as "an invention of

the devil which abrogates some of the advantages of making a disagreeable person keep his distance." That was before long-distance telephone was a practical reality.

Personally, there are times that I prefer not to be disturbed by agreeable people, and I frequently leave my landline phone off the hook. I much prefer email, which allows one to respond within one's own time management priorities.

Bierce disappeared in Mexico in 1913, so I can only imagine with considerable relish what he might have had to say about telemarketing, let alone cellphones and what they've wreaked on our culture—people in restaurants, movie theaters, business meetings, classrooms, or virtually any other social situation disturbing others, or half (at best) concentrating on the conversation while checking or sending text messages, tweeting, checking and updating their Facebook page, and the whole constant communication obsession that's called social networking, but is ironically more the death of civilized sociality.

Mobile Phones at School

Last year, when Ontario's education minister Kathleen Wynne declared that students should not be allowed to use their phones in class, my first reaction was an incredulous "you mean they are currently permitted to use them in class?"

Personally, there are times that I prefer not to be disturbed by agreeable people, and I frequently leave my landline phone off the hook.

Aside from the increasingly eclectic array of distractions from activities that should be going on in class, cellphones open up a whole new dimension of potential for cheating—Internet access, comparing notes with other students, storage and retrieval of cribsheet data—so why is the issue of banning active cellphones in the classroom even controversial? There is absolutely no constructive educational rationale for allowing active cellphone use or text messaging, let alone cellphone cameras, in school classrooms.

Since so many students pack them these days (yet another technological "necessity" that didn't exist 20 years ago), the logistics of banning the phones' physical presence would probably be impractical, but there should be zero tolerance, on pain of confiscation, for having them turned on in class, with the parent required to visit the school to retrieve confiscated devices. Another possible measure would be an automatic two-grade mark deduction if found with a cellphone turned on during a test.

Beleaguered teachers have more than enough to contend with in this era where order, discipline, and respect have fallen by the wayside without the added distraction of wireless communications and surreptitious spycams adding to the chaos.

Technology in Its Place

I'm obviously not a technology Luddite [someone opposed to new technologies], making the bulk of my living working with and writing about computers, but I refuse to become a tunnel-vision cheerleader for a *laissez-faire* [intervention-free] take-over of our lives by technology, and cellphones, while an excellent technology when used responsibly with moderation and restraint, have vast potential for abuse.

Faced with falling attendance partly due to boorish patrons keeping cellphones turned on at the movies, the National Association of Theater Owners is considering asking federal authorities for permission to jam cellphone reception in an attempt to stop annoying rings and phone conversations during films. Cellphone jamming is currently illegal in both the US and Canada. Pity.

However, new technologies under development—like a paint that can switch between blocking and allowing cellular communication by means of a radio-filtering device that collects phone signals from outside a shielded space, allowing certain transmissions to proceed while blocking others—could help persuade regulatory authorities to change their minds, and that solution might be made to work in classrooms as well as cinemas.

A Safety Hazard

The mobile device related distempers discussed in the foregoing are annoying antisocial phenomena representing a devolution of civilized manners, but there's another aspect of communication obsession that is a serious public safety hazard. In a study of 5,600 students conducted by the Children's Hospital of Philadelphia and State Farm Insurance, 89% reported seeing teen drivers chatting on cellphones—an unsafe activity not limited to teens. Insurance industry studies show that drivers in general are four times more likely to be involved in collisions while talking on cellphones.

Cellphone jamming is currently illegal in both the US and Canada.

Given actuarial data like that, why isn't cellphone use by drivers in transit not universally banned?

Partly, I suppose, because while a recent survey found that 89% of Canadians think too many motorists are driving while are distracted by cellphones, et al., only 60% said they were willing to stop using cellphones when driving.

The New York Times' Matt Richtel reported last week [in July 2009] that six years ago, the National Highway Traffic Safety Administration (NHTSA) "covered up hundreds of pages of research and warnings" about driver distraction due to cellphone because, the *Times* asserts, "of concerns about angering Congress."

Suppressed data included estimates that cell-phone-related driver distraction had contributed to 955 fatalities and 240,000 motor vehicle accidents in 2002 alone, warning that handsfree devices are no solution and may actually make things worse by nurturing a false sense of less risk from distraction.

The *NYT* report says that then NHTSA boss Dr. Jeffrey Runge reluctantly agreed not to publish the information or the policy recommendation due to "larger political considerations," i.e.: risk of angering voters who like to use cellphones while driving, as well as alienating the cellphone industry, after being told disclosure could jeopardize billions of dollars of its financing if Congress perceived the agency had crossed the line into lobbying.

The unreleased research findings reportedly included that at any given moment, more than 1 million US drivers are talking on handheld cell phones, and a 2008 survey by Nationwide Insurance found that 67% of people admitted to using a cell phone while driving.

Insurance industry studies show that drivers in general are four times more likely to be involved in collisions while talking on cellphones.

More Dangerous than Drunk Driving

Driving while intoxicated has become so much of a social taboo that most people recognize the acronym DUI (Driving Under the Influence) used by police and prosecutors, but according to a growing body of research and empirical observation, DWY and DWT are a potentially worse public hazard than DUI—and should be just as socially unacceptable.

DWY and DWT? That would be *Driving While Yakking* and *Driving While Texting* (subcategory: *Driving While Tweeting*)—the most pernicious consequences of pandemic addiction to what amounts to digital crack. John Ratey, a Harvard psychiatry professor specializing in the science of attention, told Richtel that using digital devices gives you "a dopamine [neurotransmitter; forerunner of adrenaline] squirt."

According to a UK Transport Research Laboratory study commissioned by the Royal Automobile Club Foundation, motorists sending text messages while driving are "significantly more impaired" than ones who drive drunk. The study showed texters' reaction times deteriorated by 35%, with a whopping 91% decrease in steering ability, while similar studies of drunk driving indicate reaction time diminishment of a relatively modest 12%. By that measure, DWT is three times as dangerous as DUI and should logically be treated as severely, if not more so, both under the law and in terms of social censure.

Another study conducted by the Eastern Virginia Medical School in Norfolk, Virginia, presented to the Pediatric Academic Societies in May, found teens using a driving simulator while sending text messages or searching iPod menus changed speed, steered erratically, in, some cases, ran over pedestrians, showing these behaviors clearly pose a danger to drivers and others around them. Motor vehicle accidents are the leading cause of death among people between 16 and 20, the most prolific texting demographic, with teenage drivers four times more likely to crash than older drivers even when not texting.

Update: "A driver is 23 times more likely to get into a car accident if they text when they are behind the wheel of their vehicle, according to research conducted by the Virginia Tech Transportation Institute (VTTI)," according to a news release dated 2009.07.28. Drivers are also 6 times more likely to crash while dialing their mobile phones.

Raising Awareness

It appears that a major public education and consciousness-raising effort is in order. While drinking and driving is now pretty comprehensively considered inappropriate and intolerable, texting while driving is not, with an apparent disconnect between public conviction and behavior. Reuters reported that while 83% of respondents in a nationwide US survey said DWT should be illegal, one-quarter of US cellphone users admit to texting while driving. Ongoing surveys by the NHTSA show 85% of all auto crashes and 65% of all near-crashes result from distracted driving.

Laws banning texting behind the wheel are relatively rare as yet. Only a handful of US states have full or partial bans in place. In Canada, Nova Scotia (my home province) and Newfoundland have banned use of handheld cellphones (which would include texting) behind the wheel, and British Columbia is considering such a ban.

However, while research data cited indicate that enacting laws making cellphone use while driving illegal is just as important as our now ubiquitous penalties for driving drunk, passing laws against vehicular texting may not in itself be enough. A study conducted this year by mobile technology firm Vingo found some of the worst DWT offenders living in states where DWT is already banned or ban legislation is pending. In Tennessee, an alarming 42% of drivers surveyed admitted to indulging, compared with a slightly less horrific 26% of cellphone users nationwide. Vingo found 66% of drivers aged 16 to 19—already the least experienced and most crash-prone cohort—admitted to driving while texting, and despite more states enacting bans and increased public awareness of high-profile DWT-related accidents, people still drive while texting at the same rate as a year ago.

According to the Centers for Disease Control, automobile accidents are now the leading cause of death in women under the age of 35—another cellphone-prolific, texting-oriented demographic.

The Insurance Institute for Highway Safety has determined that using cellphones, even handsfree units (which are still legal here in Nova Scotia) in voice mode, increases crash risk fourfold, and texting—which distracts visually, physically, and cognitively—increases risk sixfold. The US National Safety Council advocates banning all cellphone use by automobile operators, advising that the prudent course is to turn the ringer off and stash the phone somewhere out of reach before turning the ignition key.

Parents Need to Get Involved

Parents also need to get on the case. A survey by SADD (Students Against Destructive Decisions) and Liberty Mutual Insurance Group found 52% of teens who say their parents would be unlikely to punish them for driving while text-messaging said they would continue doing so, compared with 36% who believe their parents would penalize them.

According to the Centers for Disease Control, automobile accidents are now the leading cause of death in women under the age of 35—another cellphone-prolific, texting-oriented demographic.

The texting plague's calamitous consequences transcend the operation of automobiles. Text messaging was also identified as causing of two recent public transit disasters—a train crash in Los Angeles that killed 25 people, and a 24-year-old subway operator in Boston admitting he'd been texting his girlfriend when he rammed his train into one ahead of him, injuring almost 50 people.

This is madness. Just stop it, folks. There's no excuse.

13

Any Technology Can Distract Drivers

Simon Usborne

Simon Usborne is a feature writer at the British newspaper the Independent, *covering topics ranging from rally cars to youth football and food. An avid cyclist, he also writes the column Cyclotherapy for the* Independent.

Drivers usually believe that it is only other people who are not able to multitask when driving, and that they themselves act too smartly or prudently to get into a crash. As one driver's turn behind the wheel of a car simulator shows, however, any kind of distraction—from receiving a call to texting—slows down reaction time and causes swerving, lane deviation, and poor judgment. Operating a GPS navigation system tops the list of distracting activities in this driver's informal study.

I'm a good driver. I've been doing it for 10 years and I've never been stopped by police (well, twice), I've never been flashed by speed cameras (at least not for a few months) and, touch wood, I've never crashed—unless you count that time that, driving my C-reg [ancient] Fiesta, I pulled out into the path of a brand new Audi.

Okay, so I tell myself I'm a good driver but sometimes I'm not—and I suspect I've been getting worse recently. A few months ago, I swapped my seven-year-old brick of a mobile for a shiny smartphone that not only makes calls and sends texts but also allows me to check Facebook, take a photo of that sunset over the M40 and cue up a podcast.

I'm ashamed to admit I've done all of these things behind the wheel. I'm not alone. As the arsenal of gadgets at our disposal grows so does the temptation. That can have devastating consequences. Last Christmas Day [2008] Sheffield United footballer Jordan Robertson was driving down the M1 when he reached down to use his MP3 player. He slammed into the car in front, killing a father of five. Last Friday, Robertson, 21, was jailed for two years and eight months.

An Increase in Accidents

A study published by Heriot-Watt University suggests that three out of four crashes are caused by distractions. Top of the list was texting, something 40 per cent of people surveyed admitted to doing while driving. Other research has shown the reaction times of drivers fiddling with gadgets are 50 per cent slower than normal—and 30 per cent slower than while driving drunk.

To find out how distracting technology can be, I'm spending a day at the Transport Research Laboratory (TRL) in Berkshire. The glass and steel facility is home to one of the world's most-advanced car simulators. A Honda Civic sits on a vibrating platform and is wired up to projectors that throw a roadscape on to screens front and rear.

As the arsenal of gadgets at our disposal grows so does the temptation. That can have devastating consequences.

Dr Nick Reed, head of "human factors research" at TRL, and his team have programmed a 10-minute drive along a virtual motorway that narrows to a winding dual carriageway. When a red bar flashes I have to flick my lights to test my reaction time. The computers measure lane deviation, while infrared cameras determine how long I spend watching the road. First I complete the drive with no distractions. Then I repeat it five times while operating an array of gadgets. How bad can it be?

Making a Phone Call

For my first real test I hold my phone to my ear and have a conversation with Leana Weaver, head of trials at TRL. She has a list of questions to tax my brain. "If you see a circle with a square to the left of the circle and a triangle above the circle, is the triangle below the circle?" "Er, no," I guess as I spot a man in a black BMW undertaking me in the slow lane. Straightaway I notice deterioration in my driving but the inquisition also affects my brain. When asked to list animals beginning with "B" I give up after badger. I'm driving with one hand but Reed later tells me it's the effect phone conversations have on the mind that can prove deadly. "Our research shows that handheld and hands-free conversations cause the same level of distraction," he says. With my phone clamped to my ear I spend 15 per cent of the test with my eyes off the road (compared to 7 per cent without distraction) and I swerve more often.

> *Time spent with eyes off road*: 15 per cent
> *Increase in reaction time*: 17 per cent
> *Factor increase in lane deviation*: 1.5

Using a Smartphone

Time to whip out my iPhone. As soon as I fire up the Civic's virtual engine I start using the touch screen to perform a series of tasks. I check my work email, my own email and my Facebook account while flitting my eyes between the screen and the road. Then I launch Twitter and as I move to post something on it a people carrier pulls out in front of me. "In a driving sim in Bracknell testing how gadgets impair driving. Nearly killed a family," I tweet shamefully. The problem with touch screens is that you have to look at them because the "buttons" are never in the same place and offer no tactile feedback—it is impossible to touch type. This is reflected in the results. During my distraction-free drive I don't deviate from a straight path by more than 7cm to the left or right. But while I'm using my smartphone that figure more than doubles and I spend [nearly] half my time not looking at the road.

> *Time spent with eyes off road*: 40 per cent
> *Increase in reaction time*: 5 per cent
> *Factor increase in lane deviation*: 2.1

As soon as I fire up the Civic's virtual engine I start using the touch screen to perform a series of tasks.

Texting

You might have seen the harrowing road safety film produced in August by Gwent Police. It shows a girl texting while driving a group of friends along a busy A-road. She ploughs into an oncoming car and causes a deadly pile up. The low-budget clip became a YouTube sensation. I went into my texting test believing it would pose less of a threat because, unlike with my smartphone, I can operate my old Nokia without looking at it. Weaver dictates a series of texts over the intercom, which I tap in and pretend to send. But while my eyes-on-road figures are better than with the smartphone, there are still occasions when I have to watch the screen. The demands on my brain are distracting enough to lower dramatically the quality of my driving, which becomes clear when I have to slam on the brakes and swerve to avoid a truck that slows in front of me.

> *Time spent with eyes off road*: 30 per cent
> *Increase in reaction time*: 27 per cent
> *Factor increase in lane deviation*: 3.8

Playing with an iPod

For this test I borrow my flatmate's iPod and knock up a playlist of music you might find on a "drive time" compilation. How distracting can Chris Rea and Marvin Gaye be? Pretty distracting, it turns out. I come close to stalling when the noise in my ears masks the sound of the engine and I completely miss one of the red bars designed to measure my reaction times while I look down to skip a track. I nearly crash four times. At the post-test debrief Reed is keen to point out that today's experiments are only reasonably scientific and because, say, using a phone I performed relatively well, it should not be encouraged over another distracting activity. "You were impaired in all tests," he says. Years of campaigning mean few people would get into a car with a drunk driver. But do you challenge cabbies prodding satnavs [a GPS (Global Positioning System) device] or friends reading text messages? Reed and his team have convinced at least one bad driver to keep his eyes—and mind—on the road.

When a pair of Mercedes that have been toying with me slow down, I stupidly decide to overtake while tapping in my mum's postcode.

Time spent with eyes off road: 35 per cent
Increase in reaction time: 56 per cent
Factor increase in lane deviation: 3.4

Programming Satnav

Who hasn't tapped in a destination on the move? Satnavs are a boon but a major distraction. I fiddle with my TomTom a few times during the test and immediately notice that reaching over the dashboard to operate the screen contorts my upper body, affecting my ability to control the steering wheel. I avoid death on the motorway but things get tricky on the figure-of-eight bends, which are designed with a variable radius that requires constant adjustments to steering. When a pair of Mercedes that have been toying with me slow down, I stupidly decide to overtake while tapping in my mum's postcode. I'm all over the lane, within inches of hitting both cars at 60mph. My driving is worst in this test. "We haven't done a full study but I suspect that the satnav's fixed position is why it comes out worst than the smartphone," Dr Reed says.

Time spent with eyes off road: 30 per cent
Increase in reaction time: 27 per cent
Factor increase in lane deviation: 3.8

14

Truckers Are at Greater Risk When Texting While Driving

CNN.com

CNN.com is a national and international online news site. It is headquartered in Atlanta, Georgia, and maintains bureaus worldwide. The site relies on CNN's almost 4,000 news professionals and is updated continuously throughout the day.

While truckers are slightly less impaired than car drivers of automobiles when talking on cell phones, they do much worse when texting on their phones. A truck driver can travel long distances while taking his or her eyes of the road, and potential crashes can have devastating effects. Drivers should under no circumstances be allowed to text while operating their vehicles.

Truckers who text while driving are 23 times more likely to crash or get into a near-wreck than an undistracted driver, while car drivers face the greatest danger when dialing their cell phones, a transportation study found.

The likelihood of a crash due to cell-phone use disproportionately affected truckers in comparison with car drivers, according to the study by the Virginia Tech Transportation Institute.

Devastating Consequences

When dialing, the chance of an accident for a truck driver is 5.9 times more likely versus 2.8 times more likely for a car driver, the study found. If a trucker reaches for an electronic device, the crash risk is 6.7 times as high, while the risk for a car driver is 1.4 times as high, it showed.

Truckers only fared better while talking or listening on a cell phone, with the increased risk one time more likely compared with 1.3 times for a car driver.

Researchers viewed video footage from cameras inside of vehicles to look at how drivers engaged with the road while using their cell phones, said Rich Hanowski, director of the transportation institute's Center for Truck and Bus Safety. The study was based on research from 2004 to 2007, he said.

When dialing, the chance of an accident for a truck driver is 5.9 times more likely versus 2.8 times more likely for a car driver.

Hanowski attributed the high risk of text messaging for truckers to drivers looking at their cell phones and not at the road.

"Text messaging, as you can imagine, if you're engaged in a text message it draws your eyes away from the forward roadway," Hanowski told CNN on Tuesday.

"From the study that we did, we found that it was almost five seconds out of a six-second window that we were looking at that the driver's eyes were off the forward roadway, so that's a tremendous amount of time driving at highway speeds and a lot of opportunity in that period of time to get into trouble."

Mere Seconds Count

A news release on the study put Hanowski's point into perspective: If a highway driver takes his eyes off the road for even 4.6 seconds, it "equates to a driver traveling the length of a football field at 55 mph without looking at the roadway."

Because of the increased dangers associated with cell phone use while driving, the Virginia institute suggests that drivers avoid using phones while driving, even if they are communicating with a hands-free phone, which lessens risk, the news release said.

There's just no question; there's no redeeming factors associated with why a driver would be able to text and drive.

Researchers also recommend that newly licensed teen drivers not use phones while driving and that texting be banned.

"With regards to texting, it's really kind of a no-brainer," Hanowski said. "And I should point out we're scientists, we're not legislators, but when you see these kind of findings with regard to this level of risk texting certainly should be banned. There's just no question; there's no redeeming factors associated with why a driver would be able to text and drive."

Texting has been linked to a few high-profile crashes recently. The operator of a Boston, Massachusetts, trolley was indicted in July [2009] on a charge of gross negligence after he admitted to texting seconds before a collision with another trolley, according to the Suffolk County district attorney and a National Transportation Safety Board official. The May [2009] accident injured 62 people, the Massachusetts Bay Transportation Authority said.

In September [2008] a commuter train engineer missed a stop signal while trading text messages with a friend, leading to a collision with a freight train that killed 25 people in California, according to federal investigators. The accident injured 101 people.

15

The Trucking Industry Opposes Texting Bans

Allan P. Sloan

Allan P. Sloan is a partner at Pierce, Herns, Sloan & McLeod, LLC, a South Carolina litigation firm.

Although studies have proven that texting is a grave danger for truck drivers, trucking companies argue against a federal ban that would include on-board computer systems. Truck drivers use these systems to get updates from their corporate offices and send or receive important messages but can also access the Internet for personal use. Requiring truckers to pull over each time they use these devices will cut into profits, so companies will continue to oppose bans that include on-board computer systems.

Across the country, there has been a movement at the state and federal levels to ban drivers from sending, receiving and reading text messages while driving. The focus on text messages began in earnest over the summer [of 2009] when the Virginia Tech Transportation Institute released a study that found that drivers who text while driving have a 23 times greater risk of being involved in an accident than drivers who do not—a risk that is far greater than even drinking and driving.

Even the Governors Highway Safety Association now is on board with encouraging states to prohibit drivers from texting

Allan P. Sloan III, "Trucking Industry Looking for Exception from Texting Bans," *Pierce, Herns, Sloan & McLeod, LLC*, October 29, 2009. www.findlaw.com. Reproduced by permission.

while driving. Previously, the Association was against these bans, but changed its official policy after announcing that "texting while driving is indisputably a distraction and a serious highway safety problem."

Currently, only about half of the states have passed laws that prevent drivers from texting while driving. South Carolina is not one of them. The state, however, may be forced to adopt a texting ban if proposed federal legislation is passed.

Many trucking companies install on-board computer systems into their semi-trucks in order to communicate with their drivers while they are on the road.

The federal government wants to see a national texting ban. A bill has been introduced into Congress that would cut federal highway dollars by 25 percent to any state that did not adopt a texting ban. President [Barack] Obama signed an executive order that bans all federal workers from texting while driving when they are on government business, driving government vehicles or using other government equipment.

Texting Ban Includes On-Board Computer Systems

There also has been a push at the federal level to pass a ban that would prevent interstate bus drivers and truckers from sending text messages while driving. This ban also would include the on-board computer systems used by the majority of truck drivers—a move which the American Trucking Association has referred to as "over-kill."

Many trucking companies install on-board computer systems into their semi-trucks in order to communicate with their drivers while they are on the road. The computer systems can be used to send out important messages, new order requests and directions. Truck drivers use these systems to report their hours and status to the trucking company. The computers, however, also can be used for non-work purposes, like checking email and surfing the Internet.

While some trucking companies have policies in place that require drivers to pull over before using the computer systems, in reality this rarely happens. Whenever a truck is sitting on the side of the road, the trucking company is losing money by the minute. Given the enormous pressure on truck drivers to keep their delivery schedules, for many it is not practical to pull over every time they have to read or send a message on the computer. Instead, the drivers may keep a keyboard in their laps or nearby and use it as needed while they are driving.

There is a terrifying prospect for other drivers on the road with these trucks. It is estimated that, on average, it takes roughly four seconds for truck drivers to read one of the messages on their computers—and it can take even less time than that for an accident to happen.

The trucking industry does not want to be included in the texting ban because it is going to cost them money.

The trucking industry, however, says that the on-board computer systems are safe and do not pose a risk to other drivers. They argue that these devices require less concentration than using a cell phone or sending a text message.

While the Virginia Tech Transportation Institute did find that truck drivers using on-board computer systems have a lower risk of accidents than drivers who text, truck drivers using the devices still have a 10 times greater risk of being involved in an accident. Moreover, the on-board computer systems still take truck driver attention off of the road much in the same way that texting does, by requiring them to read and/or type out a message.

Trucking Industry Concerned About Profits, Not Safety

The trucking industry does not want to be included in the texting ban because it is going to cost them money. It will take their drivers an estimated 15 minutes every time they have to pull over to read or send a message on the on-board computer system. If they have to stop several times a day, this amount of lost time is going to result in a considerable loss of profits industry-wide.

Some trucking companies already have company policies in place that prevent some or all of their drivers from texting and/or using hand-held cell phones while driving. Additionally, there are on-board computer systems available that cannot be used while the truck is in motion or only have limited uses during this time. For example, some of the systems are equipped to have the messages read aloud to the truckers so they do not have to read them off of the screen. Safety features like these could help decrease the amount of truck driver distraction if required by all trucking companies.

The problem is that trucking companies do not have uniform policies in place when it comes to regulating truck driver distraction. And distracted truck drivers quite possibly pose the greatest risk on the roadways, given the size of these vehicles and the amount of damage [they] can do to a regular-sized passenger vehicle.

16

Truckers Welcome a Texting Ban

Laura Hampson

Laura Hampson is a writer for the Ocala Star-Banner *in Ocala, Florida.*

After the U.S. Department of Transportation banned drivers of commercial trucks and buses from texting while driving, the reactions were mixed, but a majority of drivers conceded that such a ban was necessary to keep highway and other traffic safe. When texting, drivers of trucks and buses are more likely to crash than car drivers, and a ban was needed to counteract the growing number of accidents related to cell phone use.

Sending or receiving a text message generally costs less than some pocket change. But texting while driving now will cost a lot more for truck and bus drivers—and as far as some local truckers and motorists are concerned, that's fine.

Last week [in January 2010], the U.S. Department of Transportation banned drivers of commercial trucks and buses from texting while driving. Those who violate the ban may be subject to civil or criminal penalties of up to $2,750.

Drivers who send and receive text messages take their eyes off the road for an average of 4.6 seconds out of every 6 seconds spent texting according to the Federal Motor Career Safety Administration.

At 55 mph, a texting driver is traveling the length of a football field, including end zones, without looking at the road, according to the Transportation Department.

Laura Hampson, "Truckers Onboard with Texting While Driving Ban," Ocala.com, February 1, 2010. Reproduced by permission.

Drivers Support Ban

During interviews last week at a gas station near Interstate 75, drivers expressed support for the new rule.

Drivers who send and receive text messages take their eyes off the road for an average of 4.6 seconds out of every 6 seconds spent texting.

"I can't imagine anyone would think it's intelligent to text and drive," said Lee Whitridge, a Fort Pierce woman. Whitridge said texting should be illegal for all drivers, but banning it for truck and bus drivers is a good place to start.

Richard Melton of Dunnellon said a ban on texting is "a good idea." He said it's not right that the ban applies only to truck and bus drivers, as he has seen motorists swerving on the road, distracted by their cell phones. "It should be for everyone," Melton said.

"I want people to be focused on the road," said Susan Harris of Maryland. Both of her sons have been rear-ended in accidents by drivers who were using cell phones. Harris said the ban should be for all drivers, not just truck and bus drivers.

In fact, truck and bus drivers usually are more experienced drivers because they go through training and testing for their commercial licenses, Harris said.

Thomas Perez, a truck driver for 15 years, said when drivers take their eyes off the road to text, it's dangerous for everyone. He said texting ought to be prohibited for all drivers, not just truck and bus drivers.

Perez said he occasionally sends and receives test messages while driving, but the ban and the fine will change his habits.

Distracted Driving Is Common

Perez also regularly uses an in-cab computer to communicate with dispatchers while driving, which is just as distracting as texting, he said. The Transportation Department said it plans to regulate the use of other electronic devices in the coming months.

"Text messaging should be illegal all the way around," said Larry Cairnas, a truck driver for 18 years. Truck drivers are supposed to be professional, so the higher standards are understandable, he said.

Daniel Prinz, a truck driver for 10 years, said that while he does not like additional regulations, a texting ban is probably a good thing.

Cairnas said from high in the cab of his truck that he has seen drivers using laptops, reading newspapers, putting on makeup, and just about everything else. Texting is just another thing to distract drivers, he said.

Daniel Prinz, a truck driver for 10 years, said that while he does not like additional regulations, a texting ban is probably a good thing. Prinz said he does not text while driving, but he often sees drivers "messing with their phones."

Nineteen states and the District of Columbia already have text messaging bans for all drivers, according to the Governors Highway Safety Association. Florida does not have statewide restrictions on texting.

In July 2009, U.S. Sen. Charles Schumer, D-N.Y., introduced a bill that would reduce the amount of federal highway funding by 25 percent for states that did not enact texting bans. The bill is currently in the Senate Committee on Environment and Public Works.

The government's announcement last week was followed by an unexpected announcement. According to *USA Today*, a study by the Highway Loss Data Institute found no reduction in vehicle crashes after bans on handheld cell phones were enacted in New York, Connecticut, California and Washington, D.C.

Organizations to Contact

The editors have compiled the following list of organizations concerned with the issues debated in this book. The descriptions are derived from materials provided by the organizations. All have publications or information available for interested readers. The list was compiled on the date of publication of the present volume; names, addresses, phone and fax numbers, and e-mail and Internet addresses may change. Be aware that many organizations take several weeks or longer to respond to inquiries, so allow as much time as possible.

The Alliance of Automobile Manufacturers

1401 Eye Street NW, Suite 900, Washington, DC   20005
(202) 326-5500 • fax: (202) 326-5598
website: www.autoalliance.org

The Alliance of Automobile Manufacturers supports a ban on text messaging or talking using a handheld device while driving. The Alliance advocates an approach that addresses the issue while preserving opportunities to enhance safety. It publishes its articles on driver safety online.

CTIA-The Wireless Association

1400 16th Street NW, Suite 600, Washington, DC   20036
(202) 736-3200 • fax: (202) 785-0721
website: www.ctia.org

CTIA-The Wireless Association is an international nonprofit membership organization representing all sectors of the wireless communications industry, including cellular, personal communication services, and enhanced specialized mobile radio. Info on wireless safety and driving is available on its Web site.

Federal Communications Commission (FCC)
445 12th Street SW, Washington, DC   20554
(888) 225-5322 • fax: (866) 418-0232
e-mail: fccinfo@fcc.gov
website: www.fcc.gov

The Federal Communications Commission is an independent United States government agency. It was established by the Communications Act of 1934 and regulates interstate and international communications by radio, television, wire, satellite, and cable. Articles and reports on Distracted Driving are available online.

FocusDriven
PO Box 2262, Grapevine, TX   76099
(630) 775-2405
e-mail: info@focusdriven.org
website: www.focusdriven.org

FocusDriven is a group that advocates for victims of crashes involving cell-phone-distracted driving and families of such victims. It is dedicated to increasing public awareness of the dangers of driving while using a cell phone and to promoting corresponding public policies, programs, and personal responsibility.

The Insurance Institute for Highway Safety (IIHS)
1005 N. Glebe Road, Suite 800, Arlington, VA   22201
(703) 247-1500 • fax: (703) 247-1588
website: www.iihs.org

The Insurance Institute for Highway Safety (IIHS) is a nonprofit research and communications organization funded by auto insurers. The IIHS tests and investigates ways to prevent motor vehicle crashes and works to reduce injuries in the crashes that still occur. It also publishes the traffic newsletter *Status Report*.

National Highway Traffic Safety Administration (NHTSA)
1200 New Jersey Avenue SE, Washington, DC   20590
(888) 327-4236
website: www.nhtsa.gov

The National Highway Traffic Safety Administration (NHTSA) has developed a multitiered approach to helping teen drivers become safer behind the wheel. These tiers include increasing seatbelt use, reducing teens' access to alcohol, and promoting three-stage graduated driver licensing. Articles and reports such as "Factors Related to Fatal Single-Vehicle Run-Off-Road Crashes" can be accessed on the NHTSA website.

National Safety Council (NSC)
1121 Spring Lake Drive, Itasca, IL   60143-3201
(630) 285-1121 • fax: (630) 285-1315
e-mail: info@nsc.org
website: www.nsc.org

The National Safety Council (NSC) is dedicated to saving lives by preventing injuries and deaths at work, in homes and communities, and on the roads. The NSC partners with businesses, elected officials, and the public to make an impact in areas such as distracted driving, teen driving, workplace safety, and safety in the home and community. The website provides information to both parents and teenagers about modifying risky behavior while driving.

Network of Employers for Traffic Safety (NETS)
344 Maple Avenue West, # 357, Vienna, VA   22180-56122
(703) 273-6005
e-mail: nets@trafficsafety.org
website: www.trafficsafety.org

The Network of Employers for Traffic Safety (NETS) is an employer-led public/private partnership seeking to improve the safety and health of employees and their families. NETS is committed to preventing traffic accidents that occur both on and off the job. NETS publishes a monthly electronic newsletter and makes articles on cell phone safety available online.

U.S. Department of Transportation (DOT)

1200 New Jersey Avenue SE, Washington, DC   20590
(202) 366-4000
website: www.dot.gov

The United States Department of Transportation (DOT) works to ensure a fast, safe, efficient, accessible, and convenient transportation system that meets vital national interests. The DOT operates a website dedicated to information on distracted driving, www.distraction.gov. Statistics on traffic accidents can be found at the website of the DOT's Bureau of Transportation Statistics: www.bts.gov.

Virginia Tech Transportation Institute (VTTI)

3500 Transportation Research Plaza, Blacksburg, VA   24061
(540) 231-1500 • fax: (540) 231-1555
e-mail: info@vtti.vt.edu
website: www.vtti.vt.edu

The Virginia Tech Transportation Institute (VTTI) is a research center at Virginia Polytechnic Institute and State University (Virginia Tech). VTTI seeks to save lives, save time, and save money in the transportation field by developing and using state-of-the-art tools, techniques, and technologies. Its research is effecting significant change in transportation-related public policy on both state and national levels. VTTI publishes its reports, such as "The Impact of Driver Inattention on Near-Crash/Crash Risk," online.

Bibliography

Books

Tomi T. Ahonen — *Mobile as 7th of the Mass Media: Cellphone, Cameraphone, iPhone, Smartphone*. London: Futuretext, 2008.

Naomi S. Baron — *Always On: Language in an Online and Mobile World*. New York: Oxford University Press, 2008.

Susan W. Brenner — *Law in an Era of "Smart" Technology*. New York: Oxford University Press, 2007.

David Crystal — *Txtng: The Gr8 Db8*. New York: Oxford University Press, 2008.

Charles Ess — *Digital Media Ethics*. Cambridge, UK: Polity, 2009.

Nancy Flynn — *The e-Policy Handbook: Rules and Best Practices to Safely Manage Your Company's E-Mail, Blogs, Social Networking, and Other Electronic Communication Tools*. New York: AMACOM, 2009.

Gerard Goggin — *Cell Phone Culture: Mobile Technology In Everyday Life*. New York: Routledge, 2006.

Gerard Goggin — *Global Mobile Media*. New York: Routledge, 2010.

Gerard Goggin and Larissa Hjorth

Mobile Technologies: From Telecommunications to Media. New York: Routledge, 2009.

Anastasia Goodstein

Totally Wired: What Teens and Tweens Are Really Doing Online. New York: St. Martin's Griffin, 2007.

Lisa Guerin

Smart Policies for Workplace Technologies: Email, Blogs, Cell Phones & More. Berkeley, CA: NOLO, 2009.

Julie A. Jacko and Andrew Sears, eds.

The Human-Computer Interaction Handbook: Fundamentals, Evolving Technologies, and Emerging Applications. Mahwah, NJ: Lawrence Erlbaum Associates, 2003.

Paul Levinson

Cellphone: The Story of the World's Most Mobile Medium and How It Has Transformed Everything! New York: Palgrave Mcmillan, 2004.

William J. Mitchell

Me++: The Cyborg Self and the Networked City. Cambridge, MA: MIT Press, 2003.

Michael A. Regan, John D. Lee, and Kristie L. Young, eds.

Driver Distraction: Theory, Effects, and Mitigation. Boca Raton, FL: CRC Press, 2009.

Steven Vedro

Digital Dharma: A User's Guide to Expanding Consciousness in the Infosphere. Wheaton, IL: Quest Books, 2007.

Tony Wilson   *Understanding Media Users: From Theory to Practice.* Malden, MA: Wiley-Blackwell, 2009.

Periodicals

Kristen E. Beede and Steven J. Kass   "Engrossed in Conversation: The Impact of Cell Phones on Simulated Driving Performance," *Accident Analysis & Prevention*, March 2006.

Myra Blanco et al.   "The Impact of Secondary Task Cognitive Processing Demand on Driving Performance," *Accident Analysis & Prevention*, September 2006.

Terry L. Bunn et al.   "Sleepiness/Fatigue and Distraction/Inattention as Factors for Fatal Versus Nonfatal Commercial Motor Vehicle Driver Injuries," *Accident Analysis & Prevention*, September 2005.

Larry Copeland   "Driver Phone Bans' Impact Doubted," *USA Today*, January 29, 2010.

Larry Copeland   "States Go After Texting Drivers," *USA Today*, January 24, 2010.

Birsen Donmez   "The Impact of Distraction Mitigation Strategies on Driving Performance," *Human Factors: The Journal of the Human Factors and Ergonomics Society*, vol. 48, no. 4, Winter 2006.

Birsen Donmez, Linda Ng Boyle and John D. Lee	"Safety Implications of Providing Real-Time Feedback to Distracted Drivers," *Accident Analysis & Prevention*, May 2007.
David W. Eby, Lidia P. Kostyniuk, and Jonathon M. Vivoda	"Risky Driving: Relationship Between Cellular Phone and Safety Belt Use," *Transportation Research Record: Journal of the Transportation Research Board*, 2003.
David W. Eby, Jonathon Vivoda, and Renée M. St. Louis	"Driver Hand-Held Cellular Phone Use: A Four-Year Analysis," *Journal of Safety Research*, vol. 37, no. 3, 2006.
Eugene (OR) Register-Guard	"Cell Phone Quandaries," April 23, 2009.
Ann Geracimos	"Distraction Destruction: Dialing Cell Phone, Doing Makeup Top Crash-Defying Driving Habits," *Washington Times*, June 22, 2006.
Nancy Gibbs	"Second Thoughts About Kids and Cell Phones," *Time*, March 16, 2009.
Gerard Goggin	"Adapting the Mobile Phone: The iPhone and Its Consumption," *Continuum: Journal of Media & Cultural Studies*, April 2009.
Stephanie Hanes	"Texting While Driving: The New Drunk Driving," *Christian Science Monitor*, November 5, 2009.

Richard J.
Hanowski et al.

"The Drowsy Driver Warning System
Field Operational Test: Data
Collection Methods," *National
Highway Traffic Safety Administration*,
2008.

Katherine E. Heck
and Ramona M.
Carlos

"Passenger Distractions Among
Adolescent Drivers," *Journal of Safety
Research*, vol. 39, no. 4, 2008.

William J. Horrey
and Mary F.
Lesch

"Driver-Initiated Distractions:
Examining Strategic Adaptation for
In-Vehicle Task Initiation," *Accident
Analysis & Prevention*, January 2009.

Murray Iain

"Cell Phone Accidents," *American
Enterprise*, January 2005.

Yoko Ishigami
and Raymond M.
Klein

"Is a Hands-Free Phone Safer than a
Handheld Phone?" *Journal of Safety
Research*, vol. 40, no. 2, 2009.

Melissa Jenco

"Too Young to Drive—and Use the
Phone? Legislation Would Ban Cell
Phone Use Among Those with
Learners Permits," *Arlington Heights
(IL) Daily Herald*, February 5, 2005.

Jeffrey Muttart
et al.

"Driving Without a Clue: Evaluation
of Driver Simulator Performance
During Hands-Free Cell Phone
Operation in a Work Zone,"
*Transportation Research Record:
Journal of the Transportation Research
Board*, 2007.

Jack Nasar, Peter Hecht, and Richard Wener — "Mobile Telephones, Distracted Attention, and Pedestrian Safety," *Accident Analysis & Prevention*, January 2008.

National Conference of State Legislatures, Budgets and Revenue Committee — "Special Edition: Transportation," *Mandate Monitor*, November 5, 2009.

New York Times — "Gauging Your Distraction," July 19, 2009.

Sandy Smith — "Danger Ahead! Cell Phones and Driving," *Occupational Hazards*, July 2008.

David L. Strayer et. al. — "A Comparison of the Cell Phone Driver and the Drunk Driver," *Human Factors: The Journal of the Human Factors and Ergonomics Society*, Summer 2006.

David L. Strayer and Frank A. Drews — "Profiles in Driver Distraction: Effects of Cell Phone Conversations on Younger and Older Drivers," *Human Factors: The Journal of the Human Factors and Ergonomics Society*, Winter 2004.

David Twiddy — "GPS Products Must Adapt to Beat Out Cell Phone Apps," *Arlington Heights (IL) Daily Herald*, November 29, 2009.

Internet Sources

Sherri Box   "New Data from Virginia Tech Transportation Institute Provides Insight into Cell Phone Use and Driving Distraction," *Virginia Tech News*, July 29, 2009, http://www.vtnews.vt.edu /story.php?relyear=2009&itemno=571.

The Council of State Governments   "Restricting Use of Mobile Devices in Cars," *Trends in America*, September 2009, http://www.csg.org /knowledgecenter/docs/TIA_Moble DevicesinCars_final.pdf.

Index